THE KOBE CODE

Eight Principles For Success

**An Insider's Look into Los Angeles Laker
Kobe Bryant's Warrior Life & the Code He Lives By**

BY PAT MIXON

To Kelly,
You've taught me the most important Principle in life of all.
Thank you for your love.

TABLE OF CONTENTS

SCOUTING REPORT FROM THE AUTHOR

This is an unauthorized look at Kobe Bryant and therefore, I want to set out from the tip-off that Kobe in no way had any direct involvement with this book. However, I have done my best to get it right, really stick to the letter, stay true to the core of the man, and keep the record straight.

While I have researched and pulled from a variety of sources, this book is a culmination of all the interviews and quotes Kobe has given over the years. The principles I will outline are only examples drawn from either Kobe's life or situations he has encountered. These principles only highlight how he approaches life and are only used as a writing structure to take you through Kobe's life.

Often, our sports stars are put on pedestals and marketed as heroes. That is because what they do on a basketball court is extraordinary. But these are real people. Please don't forget that. They are not supermen. In writing this book, I learned that Kobe Bryant is human. He achieves and he fails. He succeeds and he makes mistakes. But, he is to be applauded for the way he approaches his life. He truly embodies a warrior's heart.

And, Kobe is one of the most misunderstood athletes of our time. I really didn't realize the depth of this misperception by the public, and the media particularly, until I researched this book. Hopefully, *The Kobe Code* will shine a light onto Kobe's true nature, provide a new level of understanding, and possibly even change some opinions. No matter what, basketball fans are privileged to have him play and like the great gladiators Kobe idolizes, he too won't be around forever. This is a rare player and an even rarer human being. He walks with courage and lives his passion. I want to really make sure that this point isn't missed. Whether you love or loathe him, Kobe is special and we are blessed to watch him play the sport he deeply loves.

And, like Kobe, this book is on the leading edge and interactive. You'll have YouTube videos to watch if you follow links to YouTube's site directly. And, you'll have the opportunity to pop out via a link to a website and read articles from Kobe's past.

It is no coincidence that I ended up writing this book. My favorite movie of all-time is *Gladiator*. I still write often while listening to its soundtrack. And, I very much value the gladiator mentality and, most importantly, I truly believe that excellence is an attitude and a way of being. To me, Kobe is one of only a handful of individuals in the spotlight today that I feel really walks the walk. It was a privilege to learn more about him and his approach to everything he does.

So, enjoy all these insights into Kobe Bryant. If you take away even one small point from this book to use in your own life, I have accomplished my goal.

Carpe Diem.

Pat Mixon
September 2010

PREGAME

"Veni. Vedi. Vici."

Strength & Honor. Not just words from the movie, *Gladiator*, starring Russell Crowe, but a code that NBA player and Los Angeles Lakers star Kobe Bryant seems to live by. The mantra is even on his website. And, he signs all his fan letters this way.

That's because Kobe embodies everything that makes a real warrior. He possess the talent and the mindset but also the determination to win the war. He treats each game like a battle, each possession a skirmish. He is both methodical and spontaneous.

"Veni. Vedi. Vici."

That phrase is Latin for "I came, I saw, I conquered." More words the warrior Kobe follows. Again, take a look at his website, www.kb24.com. These phrases are insights into Kobe's true nature, possibly principles that guide him, and the warrior's path he walks every day of his life. This is the essence of this book.

Kobe trains like a real Gladiator, pushing his work ethic beyond anything the NBA has ever seen. He is more than dedicated, owing his grit to becoming a legend. He is at times a solo hero, a James Bond or Jason Bourne, fighting against all comers. And, Kobe has his own motivations for feeling this way.

He approaches the latest game as another night in a deadly engagement. A playoff series is all-out war. That is why Kobe plays like he lives, a Gladiator in the arena, the loser thrown to the lions. Kobe refuses to neither go quietly nor roll over. He has an unquenched thirst that drives him, fuels the eternal fire in his belly. There's a reason for this hunger which you will soon learn.

Like a solider, he is committed to total warfare, leaving everything on the battlefield. This is a "scorch the earth" mentality. Fans are left to wonder how he can be so focused, so determined, so lost in the moment. We are bewildered when a comedian like Chris Rock makes jokes at Kobe during a home game and the warrior stares into space, completely immersed, entirely focused, hearing nothing. But Kobe has his most secret weapon of all: he lives like a modern day warrior.

He lives in the present, knowing each moment, each opportunity may be his last. He trains like a rookie and prepares like a benchwarmer wanting true minutes. No one views more tape than Kobe. He watches current players and studies the legends from eras past, always with an eye for gaining the slightest edge. And, nothing gets by him. He's always looking, searching for something more, some tendency, some new wrinkle to add to his arsenal.

He is that General always assessing for the weakness, the master strategist calculating each minute detail. He is the foot solider, willing to barrel forward with brute force in the face of certain death.

From the outside, watching Kobe is like watching someone follow some invisible code, or almost like the ancient Chinese book, *The Art of War,* and he seems like he is driving himself to master it.

Kobe knows what he is up against: Real and imagined opponents; Legends; His own body; Father time; and, fan's expectations. For Kobe, opponents are to be respected. He knows when he plays that other great teams are composed of warriors as well. And, down to the last man, these are players he might not like but deserve admiration. They too are willing to die on that battlefield.

Kobe's attitude, whether an opening night in the regular season or a Game Seven of the NBA Finals is always the same. He will either walk away a victor, hoisting another NBA Trophy, or he will be carried out of the arena on his shield.

Strength and Honor, always. Veni. Vedi. Vici.

Kobe is unlike any other NBA player, possibly any other athlete of his time. He seems to live by his own code, his own principles, his own warrior ways.

In this book, you will have an inside look into both the world and mind of Kobe Bryant. But let's be clear before the game starts. *The Kobe Code* takes a unique spin on the traditional unauthorized biography. Rather than simply recap the history of Kobe, it provides insight and perspective into how he approaches his life, both on and off the court.

Additionally, by highlighting Eight Principles For Success pulled from various stages or situations in Kobe's life, this book allows you to potentially apply these simple practices to your own life. While the principles are examples only, *The Kobe Code*'s approach and structure is that of almost a spiritual guidebook, a warrior's manual, or possibly even a modern day *The Art of War* handbook.

As a result, you will not just learn the history of Kobe Bryant and where he came from but you'll understand what truly makes him really tick. You'll finally get the essence of what makes up this star player. And, once and for all, you'll understand why he has been so incredibly misunderstood.

Using life lessons from Kobe's example, *The Kobe Code* will teach you how to increase your confidence, overcome your daily challenges, live with passion and purpose, and realize your goals.

In this inspiring and practical guide, you'll learn the Eight Principles For Success that highlight Kobe's life. The number eight is significant in this superstar's life. It was his jersey number when he entered the NBA. Also, in Eastern philosophies, the number eight represents infinity.

The Eight Principles For Success are:

1. Have a Gladiator Mentality & Welcome All Challenges
2. Know What Fuels You, What Drives You
3. Fear is a Great Motivator
4. Be A Talented Overachiever
5. Accept Your Nature
6. Honor the Game
7. Master Your Craft
8. Live With Passion

If you choose, you can use Kobe's life as inspiration and use these principles to **apply** in your own life, either personal or career.

To add more depth to learning about Kobe's life, you will also discover things that the general public doesn't necessarily know or isn't common knowledge, such as:

- What is Kobe's Workout Schedule?What is his diet?
- How does Kobe spend a Game Day? You'll learn how he spends all the hours leading up to a Home Game.
- Kobe's mental approach. Learn what truly sets Kobe apart. You'll discover what Kobe does to prepare his mind and focus related to the mental aspect of basketball.
- Find out why Kobe believes in making shots, not taking shots.
- How Kobe prepares. You'll watch his Film Study and you'll see his practice sessions.
- What Kobe does off the court- where and how he spends his time & what things besides basketball interest him.

- Lastly, you'll discover Kobe's thoughts on retiring.

The Kobe Code can teach you how to walk the walk of the warrior life. It's a proven road map that you can use to achieve any goal you desire. This book is almost a spiritual guidebook, a warrior's manual, or possibly even a modern day "*The Art of War*" handbook.

And, like Kobe, this book is on the leading edge. You'll have *YouTube* videos links so you can watch Kobe and you'll have the opportunity to go to a website and read articles from Kobe's past. This is an Interactive book and so, have fun with it.

Now, are you ready to adopt a gladiator mentality and step inside the arena?

PRINCIPLE ONE

Have a Gladiator Mentality & Welcome All Challenges

" A challenge was issued to me by everyone who said I would never succeed again, that I would never win another ring or enjoy another parade. I accepted their challenge. I accepted the doubt of every one who spoke of my downfall and used their words as fuel. I have a franchise to resurrect, a city of fans to uplift." -Kobe, in 2006

This first principle is an approach to apply to all aspects of life. Looking at Kobe's past, he seems to welcome all challenges. This applies not only on the basketball court but also to life in general. It is a Gladiator mentality to welcome a challenge, not shy from it but rather, have the courage to face it.

The great Samurais of Japan demonstrated this quality to its fullest. It was a personal shame not to rise to the challenge. They knew that like a blacksmith working with iron, that the challenges under intense pressure & heat molded the individual.

Kobe has been carved and honed from his life's challenges, both on and off the court. He entered the NBA as a promising seventeen-year-old, eyes wide open and eager to learn, to become great. He faced adversity to improve, to get better on the court but his real challenges in those years were in team dynamics.

Without rehashing what has been beaten to death in the media, the Shaquille O'Neal relationship will prove to be on of the most significant relationships in Kobe's life. That's because he grew the most from it. He has said about the Shaq relationship, in an Esquire magazine feature a few years ago, the following.

"If I had to do it all over again, I just never would have said anything in the press," he says. "Some things need to remain behind closed doors. Do the fans really need to know everything? Do you need to know everything about what goes on in your neighbor's house? Do you even want to?"

While the partnership with Shaq produced three NBA titles in a row, the years that followed were the darkest days of Kobe's professional life. He had been on a team that rose to the top of what he calls "the mountain" and stayed there for three titles in a row. Kobe had learned what it took to climb that hill, the depths he had to go to make that journey. The rise to the top was sweet but the fall was equally impactful.

After Shaq and coach Phil Jackson left, Kobe and the Lakers experienced something new. The team failed to make the playoffs. Those are the bottom of the barrel times for Lakers fans, who have expectations set only at championships. Kobe was at an all-time low in the year after Shaq. He had also experienced a massive low in his personal life.

Again, without going into the details, 2004 proved to be the worst year of his professional life. An abyss he found himself drowning in. That year, Kobe had to overcome sexual assault charges stemming from an incident in a

Colorado hotel, which while the case ended long before a verdict with a dismissal due to lack of evidence, in the court of public opinion, Kobe was a convicted man. Sponsors fled like ants after the chicken at a picnic. Friends betrayed him. And, Kobe endured the unfair brunt of the blame for Shaquille O'Neal being traded from the Lakers.

Kobe was bad guy number one, in the eyes of most NBA fans and complete food for the tabloids. His marriage stability was questioned, his professional life damaged, to what most thought was beyond repair. His popularity waned so far that his jersey sales plummeted. There was barely a shoe contract.

But Kobe used his best asset to rise from the ashes. His intensity and focus provided the means to get him through his personal storm. The basketball court became his sanctuary and the starting point for his redemption.

Kobe said in 2006 as the Lakers continued on the long and winding road back to the top of the NBA that, "I will not back off until I'm back on top, back in the place where they said I could never be again. Mountains don't scare me. The LACK of mountains scares me. The climb up, the struggle for every inch of ground and every level of ascension is what feeds me."

It seems surprising but greatness needs great challenges. The climb fueled Kobe. It was the determination that he found deep within himself and began the journey back to the NBA title.

Strength and Honor. The words surround Kobe. Watch this video as further proof.

Kobe Bryant: Play with Strength. Live with Honor

Type the URL Below in your Browser to watch directly from YouTube

http://www.youtube.com/watch?v=LL5Uap85dgw

Apply the Code in Your Own Life

So, ask yourself:

Where can you summon the courage to face challenges in your own life?

Are you shying away from something that you know will be tough but has rewards beyond your wildest dreams?

Can you dig deep, let go of your inner and outer critics, and meet the challenges you face head on?

Where are you setting your own personal bar, the level of excellence you intend to achieve?

This is the way of the warrior and goes to the heart of this first Principle. Rise to the Challenge.

PRINCIPLE TWO

Know What Fuels You, What Drives You

" I have always had a purpose, a need to succeed. People who try to discourage me only add fuel to a fire that has always burned. Every phase of my life has brought me new risks and new rewards; in many ways I have always been the underdog. And through it all, through every struggle, the game has always been there. It has never left me alone."

Underdog and Kobe Bryant seem like they don't belong in the same sentence. But to understand how connected they are is to have a real glimpse into who Kobe really is. Kobe is the quintessential underdog. This goes to the heart of how misunderstood he really is by the media, by everyone, by even his most die-hard fans.

Whether true or just perceived, Kobe has felt like the underdog in nearly each phase of his life. He goes so far to call himself "an outcast." But when you learn his background, understand his childhood, you actually realize how true that statement is, and most importantly, why he actually feels this way.

Kobe's Childhood

Kobe Bean Bryant was born on August 23, 1978 in Philadelphia, Pennsylvania to Joe "Jellybean" Bryant and Pamela Cox Bryant. He is their youngest of three children and their only son. His parents gave him the name Kobe after the famous beef of Kobe, Japan. Kobe's father, Joe, is a former NBA player with the Philadelphia 76ers.

When Kobe was only six, he moved to Italy with his family when Joe left the Sixers to play professional basketball in Italy. Joe went from being a benchwarmer in Philly to becoming a star and scoring machine in Europe.

In Italy, Kobe had to adjust to a new culture and learn to speak both Italian and Spanish fluently. The learning of Latin, the root language of both Italian and Spanish, would impact Kobe's life and his principles for the rest of his life.

Kobe would learn to play hoop at only three years old and growing up, the Lakers, with Magic Johnson, were his favorite team. Family members would go so far as to mail the Bryant family videotapes of NBA games so they could watch them while in Italy. Kobe would devour these games, playing them countless times, learning moves from his heroes.

Each summer, when Joe wasn't playing basketball, the family would return to the USA and Kobe would play in basketball summer leagues, developing his skills and learning the game.

Europe is also where Kobe began his love affair with futbol, or soccer here in the US. Kobe's favorite club growing up was AC Milan.

In 1991, Joe retired from basketball and the family moved back to Philly, where Kobe would go on to attend high school at Lower Merion and become a star, catching the attention of NBA scouts, thus paving the road for him to make the jump directly from high school to the NBA, which he did in 1996.

Remember Where you Came From & Family Above All Else

There seems to be this misperception that Kobe isn't part of the African-American community. That he isn't really the same. The misbelief might have started when he returned to Philly after living in Italy for so many years. Both black and white didn't understand him, couldn't figure him out. He also didn't act like the rest of the high school kids he was around. How could he?

He was the son of a former player who had grown up in a foreign country. He could speak multiple languages. And, his game was already polished far beyond any of the inner city kids he ran up against. Kobe was playing and beating players on his dad's Italian team when Kobe was only thirteen. Think about that? He was beating pros, even if they were not NBA caliber. These were grown men.

So, when Kobe returned to the US and attended high school, he was misperceived. And, this perception simply extended on when he made the jump to the NBA. The media picked up on his background and thus came the label that he wasn't really legit, didn't really represent black America. But just as there can be a doctor or a President from any race, so can a basketball player not be a stereotype. However, it doesn't mean he isn't fully a part of that culture.

Kobe talked about this in the following quote.

"Recently I have come to visualize my place as a black athlete within our society. I've always been aware of our history, from Jackie Robinson to Sweetwater Clifton. But I never felt like I deserved to be a part of our tradition because I grew up overseas, in Italy. In that way I am very much different than many of my peers. I never truly believed that my own people wanted to identify with me.

But that's the thing about adversity: while you're going through it, you look around yourself and see exactly who it is that's rallying behind you. During my time of struggle I saw the truth. My people held me down. Their love and support became an experience for me and that experience will be with me for the rest of my life. It gave me a completely different understanding of my role. I had been wrong about my impact. Now I see that I can be a force in the lives of our youth. They look up to me for guidance and support. They have shown me that even though I grew up in Italy, I am a part of black America. The color of my skin ain't paint! It is, in fact, more than a color: it's the signifier of my culture."

Kobe realized where he came from and that he truly was not different from anyone else.

A Real Outcast

Italy is where Kobe first felt being alone, where he truly was an outsider. His feelings of being different weren't unfounded. He would be the only African-American not only in his own school, but sometimes his family would be the only ones in their entire town.

Kobe has said, "I have been an outcast my entire life. From being the only black kid in my town in Italy all the way to when I was 17 and playing in the NBA."

Learning where Kobe came from allows insight into what makes him tick, why he views the world the way he does. He joined the Los Angeles Lakers as a seventeen-year old rookie and there he was, teamed with grown men. Kobe lived with his parents in a house they got for him when he first started his career in LA. While his teammates had wives, and girlfriends and went to parties, Kobe was still a teenager.

When you put this in perspective, it is easy to see why he didn't fit in during the early years in LA, when the Lakers were Shaq's team. Kobe was a kid among men, truly a boy playing with adults. It is no wonder he kept to himself. The basketball court would be the only place he could prove he belonged.

Inner Drive

Think about what Kobe must have endured when he began his NBA career. Here he is, a teenager with talent, playing for his childhood favorite franchise, the Lakers. He must have felt inferior, entirely out of place. But like Kobe would always do, he approached his new situation with his Gladiator Mentality.

His circumstances fueled him. He had to get better. He wanted playing time, needed to be respected. But as a young man, that wasn't going to happen unless he proved himself on the basketball court. And, that is exactly what he set out to do. Kobe had to succeed. Failure really wasn't in his vocabulary.

But his dedication to improving his basketball skills, the need to get better, also alienated him from his teammates, made the media portray him as aloof, as an outsider. Kobe wasn't any of this. He simply was alone on the Lakers, was just an outcast, so different from everyone else, just like he'd been as a black kid in Italy.

About that time, he has said, "many times my drive to succeed has put me on an island all by myself because no one understood me, or they chose to misunderstand me. They chose to portray me as being something that I was not."

His drive to get better was simply misunderstood. He had to get better. In his mind, that was the only way he'd ever fit in with his far older teammates.

Kobe Bryant 's Drive on being the best

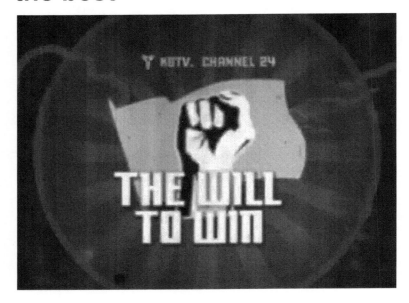

Type the URL Below in your Browser to watch directly from YouTube

http://www.youtube.com/watch?v=PUiuzqQzu4k

A Thirst To Dominate

The basketball court would be Kobe's proving ground. Naysayers doubted him, didn't think he was ready to skip college. Everyone was against him, even his own teammates, these grown men on the Lakers. That is why he came across as arrogant in those early days. But that exterior hid the real underdog behind the facade. That was the face Kobe had to put forth, the one that would keep the dogs from pouncing, the one that didn't show a weakness.

Kobe focused and set his purpose. He had a thirst to dominate, a real desire to succeed. His rookie year he would set the intention to become the best player he could be, one of the greatest ever.

He knew it would be a fight, a climb. It became his mission. He has said, "I have always had a purpose, a need to succeed. People who try to discourage me only add fuel to a fire that has always burned. Every phase of my life has brought me new risks and new rewards; in many ways I have always been the underdog. And through it all, through every struggle, the game has always been there. It has never left me alone."

This goes to the heart of this second principle. Know what fuels you and use it to drive you. Kobe exhibited this then and still does to this day. He is always the underdog, whether a bright eyed teenage rookie, the evil guy who made Shaq leave, the player wanting to be traded because he wanted to win so badly or even now, an aging superstar who should succumb to LeBron James and his Miami Heat super-team.

Kobe will have none of it but use it all as fuel. The fire in his belly still drives him. And, like always, he will prove everyone wrong.

Apply the Code in Your Own Life

So, ask yourself:

What makes you burn?

What drives you?

Who doesn't believe in you?

Are you ready to prove them wrong?

Say yes to that last question and you've adopted this second principle.

PRINCIPLE THREE

Fear is a Great Motivator

" My biggest fear is not winning another title. Fear is a great motivator."

In the summer of 2004, the media portrayed Kobe as someone who had gotten his wish. He was to blame for all things wrong in LA and most importantly, he took the heat as to why Shaq was gone and the early 2000's Lakers Dynasty destroyed.

Everyone said Kobe had made his own bed and now had to sleep in it. It was finally his team, and his team alone. And, they would rise and fall on his shoulders, his actions.

Also gone that same summer was trusted confidant and point guard, Derek Fisher, and calming influence, coach Phil Jackson.

The following season, the Lakers would fail to make the playoffs for the first time in 11 years and only the fifth time in team history. Most franchises celebrate playoff series wins, have ceremonies for Conference titles. Not Dr. Jerry Buss' Los Angeles Lakers.

An employee once asked Dr. Buss if he would give a bonus for making the playoffs. Puzzled for a moment, Dr. Buss then growled, "you'll be fired if we don't make the playoffs."

The Lakers' bar is permanently set at the championship level, locked on an NBA title. Nothing else matters, nothing else will do. For the fans of one of the most storied franchises in NBA history, anything short of a title is failure.

This is the depth of the valley Kobe Bryant found himself in the years immediately following the Shaq and Phil Jackson departures from LA. He stood there, on the valley floor, gazing up at the top of the tall mountain he had just fallen from, staring at the peak he had once stood, three times, actually. He knew what it took to reach that summit but could actually never dream how hard it would be to climb it again. In 2006, Kobe had to wonder if he would ever return to the champion podium, ever hoist the NBA trophy again.

He said at the time, "Desire is a double-edged sword. It gives you strength; it gives you motivation and focus. But occasionally, because your ambition is so great, you wonder what will happen if your goals are not fulfilled. My biggest fear is not winning another title. But fear is a great motivator. I'm determined to lead this organization back to the top. The people who once celebrated me are the same people who doubt me now. They say that because I don't have Shaq that I can't win, that it's over."

So, even our heroes have doubts. But it's what you do with your fears, with those doubts that define you. The warrior, like Kobe, uses that desire, fueled by fear, to motivate himself to start again. That is exactly what Kobe and the Lakers did. The first major move was the return of coach Phil Jackson. In his first season back, the Lakers again made the playoffs in 2006. But winning pulsed through Kobe as much as his fears. Understanding this burning desire allows insight into his actions that at times have been so misunderstood.

Although not that strong of talent surrounded him in those dark days, Kobe demanded everything from his teammates. Some rose, others caved. He said, " The only thing I truly worry about is that my drive and my will are sometimes too much for my teammates to handle. Do I expect too much from them? How can I elevate them to play with my same passion every night?"

But the warrior's nature is to push, himself and everyone, to be the best. Anything less would be his definition of failure.

In the summer of 2007, a frustrated Kobe begged Laker management to trade him. This was instigated by frustration in not being a championship caliber team, the Lakers not having the best players to go to war with Kobe. He lashed out. That fear he spoke of still seared, was still lit and he continued to drive the organization he played for as hard as he drove himself. He pushed them.

Fortunately for Laker fans everywhere, Dr. Buss and his General Manager, Mitch Kupchak, didn't panic or succumb to Kobe's pressure. They too have been to battle, know the difficult road to NBA titles and greatness.

Kobe was more concerned with being heard, seeing action by Laker management, than really following through with being traded. He wanted to know that the organization had the same goal as he: a return to the top.

Even our greatest warriors can let fear overwhelm them, and in that brief moment, in that summer, it almost did that to Kobe. But a warrior pushes through and he did. He backed off from his demands and the team turned the corner, jumping out to first place at the start of the 2007-2008 season.

But Kobe's message had been received. In February 2008, Laker management landed Pau Gasol in a blockbuster, shocking trade with the Memphis Grizzles that seemed extremely one sided, bringing the All-Star caliber Spaniard Gasol to the Lakers for what seemed like not much in return. A stroke of genius or sheer luck. Either way, Gasol was a Laker.

The quality of neither the trade nor what Memphis received is actually irrelevant to any Laker fan. What resulted is this: The Gasol trade rocketed the Lakers back into championship contention and propelled them to the NBA Finals that same year. Although the Lakers fell to the Boston Celtics in those 2008 Finals, nothing ever would be the same in Los Angeles. Kobe now had a real number two on his side, a real All-Star, a player who could actually demand double teams. He had another talented player to stand with him in battle. Gasol fit the Lakers and Phil Jackson's triangle offense like he was born to play it. His game also fit Kobe's like a glove.

But none of that happens if Kobe hadn't used his fear as a motivator. His trade demands were so misunderstood. Hopefully, you can now understand why.

Kobe demanded a return to that mountaintop. He pushed himself. He pushed his teammates. He went so far to push his owner and management. He didn't care how it was perceived, he simply demanded action. The result is three final appearances in a row since the Gasol trade and two titles. Another title looms for the 2010-2011 season.

All this is because the warrior Kobe exhibited this third principle. He used fear as a motivator, didn't let it consume him but used it to return to the top.

Apply the Code in Your Own Life

So, ask yourself these questions about your own life:

Where are you using fear to protect you?

Can you use your fear as a motivator?

What would you go for, do, if you knew you couldn't fail?

Develop the essence of this third principle. Acknowledge your fear, then embrace it, and use it to motivate you forward to conqueror your goals.

PRINCIPLE FOUR

Be A Talented Overachiever

" When I saw the movie Rudy I remember thinking, What if I worked that hard?" God has blessed me both physically and intellectually to play this game, so what would happen if I push as hard as the character in this film? I would love for people to think of me as a talented overachiever."

How do you call one of the greatest players in NBA history an overachiever? Is that even possible? Sure, he's talented. That's obvious. He may be one of the more gifted players to ever lace them up. But, he's not unique in his talent and that's why he puts overachiever in the same sentence.

What other athlete would like to be remembered as a talented overachiever? It still doesn't fit, barely makes sense. But when you really think about it, really look at how Kobe approaches every aspect of his basketball life, you start to see why.

Since Kobe has always felt like an outcast, a true outsider, that has put him in a position where he has had to prove himself on the basketball court. That's where the talented overachiever was birthed. It may not be as true today as it was in Italy, or at Lower Merion when this kid who looked black but spoke Italian and Spanish showed up acting like he could play real basketball.

And, it most certainly applied when Kobe started his NBA career, the naive, young rookie on a talented team of veterans. But, believe it or not, Kobe had to not only achieve but overachieve. His life depended on it, his NBA career required it, and the warrior inside him demanded it.

The list of talented players who never made a career in the NBA could circle the earth. The NBA is full of individuals who possessed super talents, super skills but failed to make it or stay in the NBA. It is not surprising.

Success is not just talent alone. Sure, players could get by on talent alone in high school. The superior talented ones even slipped by in college. While they found success and were coddled, this actually was there undoing. They had the wrong attitude. Their success really wasn't a result of a work ethic or an approach but relied solely on talent.

The NBA has too many players that have both talent and a work ethic. If you only have one, you can't compete. You must have both. Kobe sits on top of that list. Again, he aims not to achieve but overachieve.

For insight into the roots of his work ethic, the burning desire to be the best, we can look to a quote on the subject he made a few years back.

"I always worked hard. When I saw the movie Rudy I remember thinking, "What if I worked that hard?" God has blessed me both physically and intellectually to play this game, so what would happen if I push as hard as the character in this film? I would love for people to think of me as a talented overachiever."

This is a man who realized the talent he had but didn't rest on it. His goal wasn't just to make it in the NBA or be a decent player. He set his bar at the top.

But to achieve, he had to go to work. As he said, he always had a strong work ethic. He got this from his mother. His father, Joe, while a talented NBA player in his own right, never found success in the NBA on a major level, remaining a bench player during his years with Philadelphia. Joe even left the NBA to play in Italy for an opportunity to start, lead a team, be the showboat, the center of it all.

Kobe must have been paying attention to his father, being one of those kids that see their parent's weaknesses and drive themselves, as they grow older to never have the same ones. Some kids, at least the ones with awareness, see their parent's mistakes and never want to walk down the same path.

Kobe did this. He saw a talented father who could have been more if the man had worked harder. Joe was known as a fun guy, a nice guy but not a hard worker.

Kobe is the direct opposite. He is obsessed with working hard. This had to come in part from watching his dad. So, this is where the overachiever came from but awareness was only the first step. He had to put it to action, get to work, really push himself.

He began to develop what would become one of the greatest work ethics in NBA history. It is painful sometimes to even watch how hard he works, the extent the warrior will go to push himself. But he knows, to go to battle unprepared is futile. He knows what it takes and will make sure he is ready.

Here's what he said regarding his work ethic in the following video clips:

What motivates Kobe to have such a work ethic? Watch this.

KOBE: Live With Honor -- Work Ethic

Type the URL Below in your Browser to watch directly from YouTube

http://www.youtube.com/watch?v=k3gY48yLxig&feature=related

Now, let's take a look at his actual daily workout routine. This is a glimpse most fans never see into what this warrior really does to be ready to battle each night on the court.

Kobe's Training Philosophy: Be Prepared & Be Consistent

The main objective that Kobe has is actually not physical but mental. The real warrior's objective is to Be Prepared. Kobe seems to live by the following quote:

"Excellence is not an Act, but a Habit."

Aristotle, a Greek from over two thousand years ago, made this quote and it strikes to the heart of what Kobe believes. You aren't great some of the time. It isn't a one time or one shot thing. It is about consistency. You do it over and over again until it forms a habit. That is how excellence is achieved.

Regarding excellence in basketball, Kobe wants to have done all the work in practice, in the gym, on the track, so when he's at the game, in the flow, he simply re-enacts what he's practiced. The idea or feeling is that once out on the court, he's done it before. This is why he trains so hard, conditions his body, practices his shots until the muscles know them and why he also conditions his mind.

The other component of his philosophy is to be Consistent. This strikes to the core of his warrior mentality. As if trained by the military, he never misses a beat, never stops. He can't. No true warrior can. He has said of this philosophy,

"The thing that I tell teammates all the time is consistency. If they watch me train, running on a track, it doesn't look like I'm over-exerting myself. It's a consistency with which you do it, in other words, it's an every-day-thing. You have a program, and a schedule, and you have to abide by that, religiously. You just stick to it, and it's the consistency that pays off."

These aren't just training tips. This is a way of life, a warrior's approach.

Kobe's Fitness Objectives- Stamina, Strength & Agility

Kobe entered the league as a talented teenager but his body was more boy than man. He weighed nothing and was as lean as a supermodel. His goal was not only to become more skillful on the basketball court but also add bulk and muscle to his frame to absorb the impact he would experience over the course of an eighty-two game plus NBA season.

He accomplished this with hard work- sweat and straining that paid off. His workouts are now legendary. Kobe's workout routine is centered around stamina and strength but also agility. The other key is that Kobe wants to work not just harder but smarter. Here again, the mental approach comes into play, the warrior always being prepared, always getting the most out of each and every move, each and every moment.

Before the 2005-06 season his training regimen was described this way by Lakers Topbuzz, a Web site devoted to daily updates on the Lakers:

"Kobe . . . is now a sleek Corvette Stingray. This last off-season he altered his workout, reducing his weight to 215, and increased his wind-sprint workout to create the speed of a point guard and the stamina to prevent fading in the waning moments of a game. He is now leaner and hungry. He wants to be able to run all day and have the strength to be there and make that game-winning shot."

But the warrior's biggest asset is his willingness to push himself. You'll believe this when you see his workout schedule below. Kobe gave insight into his training schedules and the core reasons in an interview with *Men's Fitness* a few years ago.

The highlights are below in this excerpt:

> MF: Can you give us some insight into your training routine, both off-season and during the season?
>
> Kobe: During the season, I focus a lot on weight training, obviously building up my strength level as the season progresses. In the off-season, it's about getting stronger as well, more agile. Also, conditioning plays an important part in that, because you want to make sure you come into the upcoming season in tip-top shape. Then, obviously, you want to get on the basketball floor and work on your skills.

MF: In the off-season, you probably spend many more hours training, is that right?

Kobe: During the season, it's probably about four hours or so a day, with practice and extra work.

MF: So specifically though, in the off-season, what kind of weight lifting are you doing? Is it explosive movements, like plyometrics?

Kobe: Not really, it's all Olympic lifts. I do a lot of track work.

MF: So like snatches, things like that?

Kobe: Yeah, clean-pulls, dead-lifts, Romanian dead-lifts, back squats, things of that nature.

MF: One of the most impressive aspects of your game is your stamina – your ability to play so many minutes per night at such a high level. If you could pass along some tips on how to get bigger, obviously, but also to stay agile and have extra energy, would you recommend Olympic lifts?

Kobe: That helps tremendously. I think it's a combination of lifting weights and doing a conditioning program. Whatever your program is, the key is to push yourself to a level where you're hurting. You can't gain conditioning without going through it. You're going to have to feel some pain, you're going to have to feel like your lungs are burning, and you know, you want to spit up blood, that sort of thing.

MF: Sure. So what kind of cardio do you have to do – I'm imagining that during the games and practice, you get plenty –

Kobe: No, but I do a lot more. When I get on the basketball floor, it's about fine-tuning my skills, it's not about conditioning. My conditioning comes from just running, whether it's on a track, or on a field, or on the court itself, just doing suicides, or sprints.

MF: So it's just a technique thing, shooting jumpers, things like that?

Kobe: Yeah, it's something I can do over and over, so I'm in great shape. MF: How many do you shoot in a day?

Kobe: It's between 700 to 1,000 makes a day.

MF: How has your training program changed over the years? You're already becoming a veteran of the league.

Kobe: It's become more efficient. I'm not just doing a whole bunch of things. I think when you first come into the league, you kind of figure out what works best for your body, what wears down your body, what doesn't, recovery, what works best in that area. I've been in the league 10 years, 11 years now so I know exactly what works and what doesn't work for me.

MF: Do you have any training tips, aside from Olympic lifts, that you'd recommend to younger basketball players?

Kobe: The thing that I tell them all the time is consistency. If they watch me train, running on a track, it doesn't look like I'm over-exerting myself. It's a consistency with which you do it, in other words, it's an every-day-thing. You have a program, and a schedule, and you have to abide by that, religiously. You just stick to it, and it's the consistency that pays off.

MF: If you could pinpoint one part of your game – and this would really be nitpicking – what would it be?

Kobe: It depends – I usually make those evaluations at the end of the season, along with Phil (Jackson) and the coaching staff, and break down the season and how I progress, and how I evolve as a player, go into the summer with a plan, exactly what I need to work on.

MF: So that's every summer? You break your game down?

Kobe: Oh yeah. You have to…

Read the entire article by typing the URL below into your Browser.

http://www.mensfitness.com/exclusives/206

Kobe's Daily Workout Routine

According to *Inside Hoops*, Kobe follows what is called the "666 workout" which was developed by Michael Jordan's former trainer, Tim Grover out of Chicago. The workout breaks down as follows: 6 hours a day, 6 days a week, 6 months. The 666 consists of:

2 hours of running
2 hours of basketball
1 hour of Cardio (boxing, jump rope, etc)
1 hour of Weights which are listed below:

Day 1 & Day 4:

Bench press
Lat pull-downs
Incline press
Military press
Abdominal crunches

Day 2 & Day 5:

Lateral dumbbell raises
Bar dips
Tricep press-downs
Bicep curls
Abdominal crunches

Day 3 & Day 6:

Back squats/Front squats
Leg curls
Leg extensions
Calf raises
Abdominal crunches

(Note: Remember, Kobe is a world-class athlete. The above schedule is not something the average Joe can follow from day one. This is an "ideal" training schedule only.)

Even Kobe has varied it over the years, in recent years altering his training regime to improve his speed. So, use the above only as a guide and a standard for your own workouts.

Kobe's Diet

Exercise is only one component of a world-class athlete getting the most out of his body. Like a Michelangelo statue, Kobe needed to sculpt his body not only from weights but also by adhering to strict diet, designed to give him speed, energy and endurance.

His diet was created to support the tremendous calorie consumption his training and games demanded. He also wanted to remain lean and keep his body fat composition at a minimum. Kobe achieved this by eating the following diet and spreading out his meals this way:

> meal #1: breakfast (egg whites, toast, protein fruit shake)
> meal #2: snack (fruit or salad)
> meal #3: lunch (turkey sandwich, steamed fish with brown rice, veggies, water)
> meal #4: snack (fruit, salad or low-fat yogurt)
> meal #5: dinner (baked/steamed lean chicken breast, steamed broccoli/veggies, etc..)

(the above is a sample day only. He did state to Esquire Magazine that he eats five times a day.)

For more info on his eating habits, check out the following video:

Kobe covers a lot of ground in Santa Barbara including Diet

Type the URL Below in your Browser to watch directly from YouTube

http://www.youtube.com/watch?v=Ohz7P6TE1CM

Kobe Training Videos

Kobe has talked multiple times about his training regime. Additionally, the videos below are a glimpse at Kobe actually working out. Here are some of them:

Typical Kobe Bryant Workout

Type the URL Below in your Browser to watch directly from YouTube

http://www.youtube.com/watch?v=3J0bZe6iyrl&feature=related

Kobe Early Morning Workouts

Type the URL Below in your Browser to watch directly from YouTube
 http://www.youtube.com/watch?v=d3D6t0YQwOo&feature=related

Kobe's Influence

Kobe's warrior work ethic has impacted far more players than you would expect. The 2008 Olympic team got treated to his training regime first hand as they prepared for the games in Beijing, China.

But his former teammates also have been affected. One of them, Caron Butler, currently with the Dallas Mavericks, played with Kobe in LA when he came to the Lakers as part of the Shaquille O'Neal trade to Miami. While still with the Washington Wizards, Butler talked about Kobe's influence. He said at the time the following:

"I say that's the best thing that ever could have happened for me personally for my career," Butler said. "To play alongside a guy [Kobe] like that, see his preparation, see what it takes to get to that level, that's why I was able to be so good in Washington because I took everything I learned from him under his wing."

Butler played in 77 games in 2004-05 with the Lakers. He averaged a then career-high 15.5 points and then career-high 5.8 rebounds. His free throw shooting improved, too.

"Work ethic," Butler said. "Kobe comes to the gym 6:30, 7 in the morning, gets shots every day, a rhythm. Afterward hits the weight room, works out in the summer, studying film, critiquing guys, watching their tendencies, picking things up ... Just studying the game with him taught me a lot."

Read original article below:

Type the URL Below in your Browser.

http://mavsblog.dallasnews.com/archives/2010/02/caron-butler-grateful-he-was-kobe-bryant.html

Even players from other sports have been affected by Kobe's work ethic, this warrior's mentality. Recently, Major League Baseball star and St. Louis Cardinal All-Star, Albert Pujols, had the opportunity to meet Kobe along with Pujols' son. The meeting would be memorable for both father and son. Below is the video clip of Pujols talking about the encounter with Kobe.

Albert Pujols on meeting Kobe Bryant

You Tube

Type the URL Below in your Browser to watch directly from YouTube

http://www.youtube.com/watch?v=X0CIXfZA14s&feature=related

Apply the Code in Your Own Life

One can definitely follow both Kobe's training and diet and apply this to your own life. But remember, his regime and food have been specially designed and tailored to his own individual body and goals. It is more important to view his mental approach and the dedication he puts into being the best.

So, ask yourself these questions to apply the Kobe Code in your own life.

Can you approach your new goal by Being Prepared?

How can you be more Consistent in approaching your goals?

Can you push your talent further?

Where are you holding back and not pushing yourself harder?

What areas of your life can you be an overachiever?

Be consistent and emulate even a piece of Kobe's vaunted work ethic and you will have the essence of this fourth principle. And, you too can strive to be that talented overachiever in everything you do.

PRINCIPLE FIVE

Accept Your Nature

" It's OK to be different than others. It's OK to want to be the best. It's OK to feel like a loser if you don't win it all, and it's OK to bounce back with a stronger will, a deeper sense of determination, and a desire to destroy your opposition. I have learned that it is OK for me to be me, and what being me entails."

Along with being an outcast, Kobe has been criticized much of his life for being so driven, so narrowly focused. At times, he has been attacked for this, his nature to succeed.

The average person simply doesn't understand. Most people live their lives in mediocrity, accepting the middle ground. But not the warrior. This person accepts their true nature and strives to be better. It is not just words when Kobe says he wants to "destroy your opposition."

No solider, no warrior can go into battle without an edge. In the real world, that weakness is trained out of soldiers. For athletes, this has to be learned. However, just like not everyone can dunk a basketball, certain people possess an inherent competitiveness, a deep down killer instinct. This part might get trained, like a muscle but it is there from the beginning. And, like a great pianist, this will to win must simply be cultivated. But society doesn't always understand soldiers or warriors and, in the case of Kobe, doesn't quite understand him, either.

Because of this, he has always felt different, and, in reality, he is. He is an uncommon man in a common world that accepts common achievements. To really excel, one has to push, not just move, beyond these societal bounds. He talked about how others viewed him and, what he thought of them. He said the following:

"I have faced so much criticism for my drive that at times it has alienated me from the majority: the people who are comfortable with second place, the people who hate against me because I am not.

You know these kinds of people; they are the ones who fear winning, the jealous ones who envy and try to sabotage. They are the people who have been telling me I couldn't win all my life.

Many times my drive to succeed has put me on an island all by myself because no one understood me, or they chose to misunderstand me. They chose to portray me as being something that I was not."

But Kobe's competitive nature is unlike not only most people but also rare even in the NBA. Only a select few players have possessed this killer instinct to the extent Kobe exhibits. Jerry West, Larry Bird, Michael Jordan and Magic Johnson all displayed this need to win. At anything, and, everything. Whether on the court or in a game of cards, their competitiveness always showed. It is said that these types of players can't lose at anything. And, it is true. Kobe refuses to lose, most especially, on the basketball court.

The sneer, the clenched teeth, these aren't an act but the face of a warrior. It is hard to understand, sometimes even harder to watch. It appears he isn't having fun but this is the exact opposite. He loves the game. It is the competitiveness, the drive, that fuels him and he enjoys every second of it, on and off the court. This is his time, his place of fun, whether he is running sprints in the fog of an early morning workout or rising up to sink a jumper to win a NBA Finals game. It is the battle that matters. Always.

Kobe talked about competition at his 2010 Basketball Academy. He said that it all started growing up. "I'm pretty brutal. It has a lot to do with the way I grew up...I had a lot of cousins growing up, we were all competitive...Even with a video game, always wanted to win...It's the same way with teammates."

Kobe talks about competition & "Sacrificing for Gold" during 2008 & Team USA looking to win the Gold Medal

Type the URL Below in your Browser to watch directly from YouTube

http://www.youtube.com/watch?v=d3D6t0YQwOo

Kobe finally found others like him, not where you would expect. Sure, there are a few players in today's NBA that have the streak of competitiveness that Kobe possesses. But everywhere else, he never sees his true nature, the inner warrior.

Until the time a few years ago that he visited Nike headquarters in Oregon. There, he met other top athletes from an array of sports that were also sponsored by Nike. These individuals endorsed the footwear company and its products just as Kobe does.

When Kobe walked into the room for the group meeting, he finally felt home. He was finally among other true warriors whose spirits burned as deep as his. The feelings overwhelmed him. He had never felt this way before, never had peered into the eyes of other athletes and saw...himself.

He said of the experience. "There are certain kinds of people that are purely driven. I can tell who they are simply by looking at them."

The meeting transformed Kobe, meeting the likes of great tennis, golf, baseball, and other top athletes. It was a momentous day for the lifelong outcast, the lone warrior. There were others on the same path to greatness that he now walked.

But what Kobe really learned from the Nike experience was that being him was okay. He learned to accept his true nature. He realized that being a true warrior did set him apart from the rest of society but he wasn't wrong for being that way nor alone.

Kobe applied this core principle to his own life. He accepted his true nature, finally stop denying it, trying to hide it. He quit pushing against the media and a funny thing happened. He became more liked. His fan base grew again.

Now, he sits at the top, not only a champion but one of the top players in the NBA, actually the most popular player worldwide. His jersey outsells every NBA player, even LeBron James.

Kobe said that he learned it was "OK to be different than others. It's OK to want to be the best. It's OK to feel like a loser if you don't win it all, and it's OK to bounce back with a stronger will, a deeper sense of determination, and a desire to destroy your opposition. I have learned that it is OK for me to be me, and what being me entails."

That was the key. He learned it was okay to be him. That is what a true warrior does. He accepted his nature and it has finally made all the difference. Kobe understands how he is and even his nickname, The Black Mamba, personifies it.

He spoke about how he got his nickname at his 2010 Basketball Academy. He said that it is one of his favorite snakes. He's a thrill seeker. Loves sharks, black mambas, and king cobras. He's intrigued and fascinated by how animals behave and hunt. Black Mamba caught his attention. He said that when he was talking trash back and forth with ex-Laker Ronny Turiaf, he warned Turiaf to back off or the "Black Mamba gonna come out." Turiaf ran with the name and from then on, Kobe was the Black Mamba. And, he still is.

Kobe also knows he can only be the best Kobe he can be. He understands he is just a man, knows he is only human. He is the last person to say he is perfect.

Don't believe that? Watch this video.

Kobe Bryant on Nobody's Perfect

Type the URL Below in your Browser to watch directly from YouTube

http://www.youtube.com/watch?v=xao5GQysVul

Apply the Code in Your Own Life

So, ask yourself:

How can you apply this principle in your own life?

What or who are you pushing against?

Are you trying to conform, rather than develop who you truly are?

Are you afraid to be different?

Are you afraid to chart your own course for your life, play your own game?

Can you let go of what others think and focus only on what you want?

Be willing to really accept yourself, your true nature and you will be embracing this fifth principle.

PRINCIPLE SIX

Honor the Game

"Because the game has given me so much I know that I must give it the respect it deserves. I must work hard to master it, to show it my appreciation for all it has done for me as a person, as a man."

Maybe it was all the videos Kobe's grandparents sent him while he lived in Italy. Or, maybe it was watching all of the games his dad played in. Possibly it was actually playing against some of his father's Italian teammates. Or, maybe it was because he was alone, like many kids growing up, playing at home, just Kobe and a basketball, the sun going down as he shot in his driveway. Somewhere along the way, as a kid, Kobe fell in love with basketball. It's a love affair that hasn't ended but only deepened over time.

If you extract each of the characteristics that the great basketball players of all-time have possessed, the checklist starts to look like this: Talent, skills, drive, killer instinct, and work ethic. But there is another trait above all else and each warrior also has it. And, you can't teach it. It's the love of the game.

Love of the game is the key ingredient, above all others.

When Michael Jordan was a young player in the mid-1980's, he put into one of his early Chicago Bull's contracts a clause that was unique for the time. Since NBA players are basically indentured servants, most owners have in player's contracts that they can't play basketball outside of team approved events. This means in summer, no pickup games, no random playing. The team doesn't want the player at risk, doing something outside of a team organized practice that the player could get hurt. The team has millions of dollars invested in each player. Especially its stars. But MJ didn't understand why he would be restricted to play the game he loved. He wanted to be able to play whenever or wherever he wanted. He wanted freedom to play the game he loved.

So, in that early contract, he added the clause that came to be called the "Love of the Game" clause.

We are told that Kobe has the same clause in his current contract. He loves the game he plays and will not be limited. This is a true warrior's spirit. To be great, you must have love. But the love extends further. It goes to Honor.

Kobe believes in the warrior's life, walks the gladiator's path each and every day. But Strength and Honor don't just reside on his website but in his heart.

Honor the game. This is what Kobe believes to his core. He understands what he has gained from the game and he must give back. This means not just in how he plays but in how he approaches his profession. Honor is the true warrior's calling.

<u>First Love</u>

Kobe might have been introduced to basketball while in Philly when his dad still played in the NBA for the 76'ers. But that was simply dating, checking the game out. No, Kobe's love affair really began in Italy. He's been bewitched ever since.

Those videotapes would prove to be more than just watching recent games, just catching up on how Kobe's favorite team, the Los Angeles Lakers, and his favorite player, Magic Johnson, were doing. No, those tapes were blueprints. They were lesson plans. The way of each warrior is to study and learn, to constantly improve. For Kobe, those early videotapes proved to be basketball instructional videos.

When each tape would arrive in the mail, Kobe would play those tapes over and over again, until a family member said, "the tape was going to break." It wasn't just about entertainment or not having anything else to watch. Those tapes began Kobe's true love of the game and, most importantly, how it was played. And, the reason he excels, is that the love of the game has never ended, and continues to this day.

Kobe was quoted on this subject recently saying, "As I've gotten older and actually become famous I realize that it's not what I thought it would be. But this is a good thing. Because it means that, in my heart, I never played the game for "spotlight" reasons. I played because I loved it."

This will be a love affair that will last Kobe's entire life. Basketball is both his first and last love and will define him forever.

At his 2010 Basketball Academy this past summer, Kobe talked about one of his favorite childhood memories. He said that everything for him goes back to basketball. The greatest Christmas gift he ever received was at age six when he got a real, official NBA leather basketball. He slept with it and never let it go. And, he made a point to say how important it was that it was a real official ball. Now, that's love.

Kobe's love of basketball goes so far as pushing through injuries and playing hurt. It's all about love. Watch this video and you'll understand how much he loves the game.

Kobe Bryant on How Love gets Him Through Pain

Type the URL Below in your Browser to watch directly from YouTube

http://www.youtube.com/watch?v=iK56xiTPBds&feature=related

Film Study

There isn't a player in today's NBA who watches more film that Kobe. He might watch more tape than anyone in history. He is like an obsessed NFL coach, studying game tape until his eyes bleed.

Kobe is like a human surveillance camera, always looking, always assessing. He will watch footage of players on both offense and defense, searching for tendencies, breaking down moves. He'll study a team's sets, try to uncover a slight edge, the smallest of advantages. But, Kobe will also study himself on film. This is one of the differences between the warrior Kobe and everyone else. That's because Kobe truly follows another warrior principle: "Know thy self."

Kobe truly believes this. Most people don't like or want to see themselves on film, especially having to be critical of themselves. But Kobe is transparent to himself in that he almost watches himself on film like an independent observer.

There is almost an eastern religion feeling to this. He is that third party observer, assessing his own play like any other player, even though he is watching himself.

There is true magic in this practice. Kobe is able to detach from his own ego and really see what he is doing right, and wrong. From this point of neutrality, he is then able to correct it. This is a warrior's practice. Detachment. Kobe displays this trait when watching film.

PHD in Basketball

But Kobe also watches footage of old legends, from all eras. He is a student of the game. He might have skipped college but he still graduated with top honors from Basketball U. You might say he actually has a PHD in Basketball. Kobe's profession is basketball and he is like a brain surgeon, highly studied and highly practiced at his job.

But why does he look to the past so much, watch so much tape of old players? Simply put, there is gold to mine.

Kobe has said the habit started back in Italy, with those tapes he would receive from the US. He would watch a game, see a move, and then go outside and practice it until he could literally mimic it to perfection. If it took ten minutes or ten hours to master, he didn't care. Then, he'd spot another move he liked and do it again. This was a constant for him growing up and learning the game.

In a strange way, Kobe is a trained mimic. He can copy any move from any player but in many cases, make it even better. He can emulate most of the greats of the past. His game has a little sprinkle from a slew of legends. If you really wanted, you could break down his game and classify each move and where it came from. And, from whom.

Kobe can actually do this. He can tell you who had the best jab fake. Who had the best spin move. Who had the quickest pull-up jumper. He knows it all. And, if the move is included in his game, he can tell you who originated it and who perfected it.

He's like a walking almanac of basketball history. You can quiz him about a game in the past or a player and he can recite down to the minute on the scoreboard the details of the exact game. He knows it all. Not just who won the title or in how many games but everything.

One of the main reasons for his basketball history proficiency is that he's seen more footage than the NBA Hall of Fame. Kobe is one of the few people on the planet who has gone out of his way to see games that almost no one else has. He makes a point of it. That's because it thrills him. He loves it.

ESPN.com recently ran an article on how Kobe "imitates greatness." It is well worth the read.

To read the ESPN article in detail, type the URL below into your browser.

http://sports.espn.go.com/nba/playoffs/2010/columns/story?columnist=macmullan_jackie&page=kobefilmstudy-100604

Kobe Bryant's amazing film study

Type the URL Below in your Browser to watch directly from YouTube

http://www.youtube.com/watch?v=3yxJjwgJZ84

Kobe Bryant on Great Role Models

Type the URL Below in your Browser to watch directly from YouTube

http://www.youtube.com/watch?v=40BFml5eq3o

Home is the Basketball Court

So, where does an outcast find a sanctuary? Where does the warrior go for solitude? For Kobe, the basketball court is his temple. It is his place to escape. No matter what is going right, or wrong in his world, he can always find peace on the court.

It can be a playoff game or simply being alone in the gym shooting jumpers. Makes no difference because the one place on earth that Kobe finds true joy, and real peace, is in on that hardwood. Basketball is both his mistress and his psychologist.

He said once, "The game has actually helped me cope with it. It has helped me win. Not in terms of the points scored, but in terms of the struggles that I have overcome."

The games helps him deal, relax, vent. He added, "When I needed someone to lean on, a place to vent, a place to celebrate or a place to cry, the game became all of these things for me."

That's why he honors the game so much. Does nothing but respect it. He pushes himself because he doesn't want to cheat the game he loves. He knows what the greats have given. And, he understands what is truly required.

So, when he crosses over those white lines, when he's laced up his shoes and slipped on his uniform, he's transformed into that warrior. Everything in the real world slips away, disappears, even for that brief moment in time because on the basketball court, Kobe is home. He is the embodiment of this Principle. He loves the game and honors it with every ounce of his being.

Apply the Code in Your Own Life

Ask yourself these questions:

Do you truly love your profession? Do you burn to do the work you love?

What did you love to do as a kid?

What would you do if money didn't matter?

If you had all the money in the world, then what would you choose to do?

Are you a real student of your profession?

Are you giving 100% of your effort to become the best at what you do?

Are you living with Honor in what you do?

If you would push yourself, really live by this six principle, you could transform your life.

PRINCIPLE SEVEN

Master Your Craft

" What thrills me most about the game is the purity of it and the chance to master it. The process, the work, the beauty of it has always inspired me."

Master your craft. Isn't this at the core of every successful person? Aren't the greatest of warriors masters at what they do?

Kobe is no different. This is why becoming a master seems to be essential to Kobe's core spirit. The mindset alone to master his sport is actually the first pillar of this principle.

There is a great eastern quote that says the journey of a thousand miles begins with a single step.

So, how does one become a master? Take the first step. Then, the next. But it all starts in the mind.

Kobe made the decision early on in his basketball career to master the game. He knew it would take focus, dedication, and hard work. But, Kobe's approach to become a master isn't a burden to him when you consider the following quote:

"What thrills me most about the game is the purity of it and the chance to master it. The process, the work, the beauty of it has always inspired me."

The process thrills him. Don't we all wish we could describe our profession, our work, in that way? Isn't that what we all want to feel in our daily activity?

Basketball fills Kobe up, gives him that energy to push through the hard times, the tough workouts. That is because he is connected to his inner self, his true calling, and the depths of the passion fires that burn in his belly.

The key here is that to be a great warrior, you must commit yourself to master your craft. And, the journey begins in your mind. First you must adopt this warrior mentality, then take the action.

However, to take action without the mental component in place first will waste a great deal of time and effort. But, if you focus and decide what you truly want, you will be in alignment with your deep desires and then everything will conspire to help you. The point to understand is that you become a master over time.

An author doesn't write a novel in one sitting. In fact, the joke is that you write a novel one day at a time. But, after many days, months, and sometimes even years, you do end up with a completed novel. You climb the mountain one step at a time to become a true master.

Kobe too didn't master basketball overnight. He wouldn't even consider that he has gotten there, even now, at this point in his career.

This too strikes to the heart of this principle. Never settle on where you are at but constantly push yourself to get better, learn more.

And so, the intention to master your craft is more about the journey than the destination. This may sound like some Eastern philosophy mumbo jumbo or possibly something Phil Jackson might preach. And, you'd be right.

That's why Kobe would never say he has mastered his sport. To him and the real warrior, the goal is to strive. To get better each and every day, each and every play, each and every season. The great warriors never reach the end. If they did, they would die. The fires in their bellies would be extinguished and the passion would leave. If this happened, it would be time to stop, time to end it.

Kobe is nowhere near stopping, not even close to being done. Even though he now sits on the top of the NBA mountain, he still feels like he has much, much more to accomplish. Master his craft. That is the philosophy, that is the way.

What goes through Kobe's mind is this. Keep working. Get better. Assess and correct. For example, he now wants to improve his post game. He desires to continue to improve his outside shot's accuracy.

At the end of each NBA season, Kobe and his training team set out to assess his game and determine what both his body and mind needs for the next season. They create a goal sheet that will be the blueprint of Kobe's work over the summer.

Kobe learned this process when he became a Laker. The Lakers always have what they call an "Exit Meeting" with each player within days of the season ending. Even Kobe Bryant has this meeting with Phil Jackson and his staff.

Jackson goes over the season, what worked and what didn't. He and his staff talk about the upcoming campaign and what changes they would like to see in each player.

For Kobe, Jackson has goals of leadership as well as on the court areas for improvement. Kobe takes these comments, processes them into his own warrior mentality, and then gets with his personal training team to get to work in the off-season. Many of Jackson's points will make it on Kobe's personal goal sheet for summer. Kobe will integrate both what Jackson has suggested as well as make his own modification and additions to his game.

This is how the warrior approaches his craft. He knows what he is good at and where his weaknesses lie. And, most importantly, before any physical action has been done by the warrior, the mind must be focused in the direction of improvement. This is step one of mastering your craft.

Prepare & Out Study Your Opponents

The second step on the journey of mastery is to prepare and out-study your opponent. Real and imagined foes are out there, waiting for Kobe. He tells himself this all the time, uses it to fuel his fires. It is almost like gasoline for your car, it keeps him going.

Someone once said success is the convergence of preparation and perspiration. Kobe has never quoted this phrase but his actions speak otherwise. He prepares unlike any other player in the game today. While we have already covered Kobe's physical training in detail, he also brings his warrior mentality to the mental approach to basketball.

If you believe that today's NBA is only a physical game, based on unique talent, the most conditioned athletes in the world going at it, head to head, on the hardwood, think again. To really excel at the highest level requires preparation. This means studying. And, Kobe didn't enter the NBA a preparation maniac to start. Sure, he was already dedicated to his sport, wanted to be the best he could be, but he has learned new skills along the way.

He freely admits that Laker coach Phil Jackson has had probably the most impact on his mental approach to the game. Along with Jackson, Kobe also relies on Lakers Special Assistant Coach, Tex Winter, the inventor of the Lakers' triangle offense. Kobe spoke about the influence of both men on his mental approach to the game. He said:

"The fears I have are soothed a little by the presence of Phil Jackson. Simply put, he is the best coach I have ever played for. Everything I have learned about the game can be traced to him and Tex Winter. They teach the game at such a deeper level than X's and O's. The game is a rhythm, a dance. Phil and Tex have taught me to feel the game. To think the game without thinking, to see without seeing. They taught me how to prepare. How to conceptualize the spirit of my opponents and attack them where they are weak. I've seen how prepared PJ gets before games, and as the on-court leader he is trusting me to do the same. So I do all the things he has taught me to do before tip-off and once the ball is in the air my mind is at ease and my body is ready to play."

It is no coincidence that the game's greatest warrior, the true gladiator Kobe Bryant ended up partnered with the game's most successful coach who goes by the reputation known as the Zen Master. For a man like Kobe, who seems to live by his own warrior code and principles, he needed Jackson as much as anything in his life.

Phil Jackson is successful because of his own mental approach to the game. At this point, with 11 NBA titles to his name, Jackson is the game's greatest coach of all-time. It is undeniable. The naysayers used to say he was a good coach but only because he had been blessed with great players. The line went that anyone could win a title with Michael Jordan or Shaquille O'Neal or even Kobe Bryant.

But really? MJ never won until the Zen Master arrived on the scene in Chicago, implementing both the famed triangle offense and his infamous mental approach to the game. Regardless, Jordan flourished and dominated.

Jackson showed up in LA with Shaq and Kobe having already spent nearly four years together without a title.

The season Jackson arrived, the Lakers won the title and made it three in a row.

Finally, when Jackson returned to the Lakers to re-team with Kobe for a final assault of the mountain, Kobe was just climbing out of the gutter he had fallen into after the end of the Shaq in LA years.

It is indisputable the impact Jackson has had. But, detractors still pointed out that Boston Celtic legendary coach Red Auerbach was the best coach ever. Until Jackson surpassed Auerbach's 9 NBA titles, the argument stuck.

But people forgot that Auerbach also had all the great players in his day as well, long before free-agency could change the complexion of your team. The Celtics owned the 1960's but they were like the New York Yankees of the 1920's. They got the best players.

But finally, Jackson has silenced all the critics by not only overtaking Auerbach but shooting past him now with 11 titles and counting. And, there is no reason he won't get possibly another one this year.

And, count on Kobe to do everything in his power, give every ounce of his being in the arena to make that title hope a reality. And, for the warrior, it starts with the principle of preparation.

To add to Kobe's beliefs on the importance of preparation, he talked about the subject at his 2010 Basketball Academy this past summer when a camper asked him if he had any superstitions about the game. Kobe said no. That he isn't superstitious at all. He's never been. He prepares, does his work. Other players had routines but he noticed in high school that if someone was thrown off from their routine and then during the game, their shot didn't go in. After the game, they would say it was because they didn't follow the routine. Kobe didn't like that and said to heck with it. He does whatever he feels like on game day, trusts himself. He isn't superstitious because simply believes in preparation.

Know Your Opponent Better than They Know Themselves

To go to battle, one must be prepared. This philosophy can be seen throughout history, in the blueprints of famous military victors, and even in the sport of basketball. The famous book *The Art of War* is recognized by military strategists, business people, and even athletes as the quintessential guide for victory. One of the key principles that fits in *The Art of War* is the following:

> *Know Your Opponent better*
> *than they know themselves.*

The key to using this principle is that the great warrior knows both his opponent's weaknesses and strengths.

It is obvious to study a player's deficiencies and then exploit them. That is what basketball is all about. A taller guy will take his smaller opponent down low and take advantage of the height difference. A quicker player will fake an outside shot and blow by the slower opponent for an easy bucket. Even on a team scale, in the NBA, the game is always about match-ups and adjustments. For example, the Lakers will use their height advantage to pound a smaller opponent.

But what about your opponent's strengths?

This is the key element of the warrior's approach and one Kobe utilizes to perfection. He constantly watches film and studies what his opponents love to do, what their favorite moves are. Then, he wants to neutralize or defend that move. He wants to prevent the opposing player from getting to a favorite spot. He attempts to keep a post up player out of the paint. He gives a smaller, quicker guard extra space on the perimeter.

Kobe knows when and how to do this because he has seen it countless times and in endless situations on film. He knows what the other player wants to do and won't let him.

Why know your opponent's strengths? Because if you don't let them use what they love, they get frustrated. And, Kobe knows a frustrated player is a weakened player. That is a four-point switch. Not only has Kobe prevented the player from using a go-to, favorite move, but because he has prevented it, the other player is frustrated.

That is what a warrior does. Beats you not only physically but mentality. And, that all starts with preparation and study.

Film Study

Kobe has always been watching basketball games, going back to when he would rip open the videotapes his grandparents sent him in Italy. Each new tape was like a Christmas gift, the young Kobe anxiously awaiting new footage to immerse himself into. He would watch those tapes and learn. He would run out to his basketball court and practice the moves, then return for more on those tapes.

Nothing has changed with the grown-up Kobe. He still loves watching basketball games, whether himself or opponents. Sure, he now watches on his laptop and his personal training staff includes a guy whose only job is to edit video of games and opponents, breaking down the footage for Kobe to digest. He breaks down his own moves as much as assessing an opponent or even watching players from other eras, the legends of the game.

Kobe is always looking to refine and improve. This is the way of the warrior and at the heart of preparation. He not only won't be outworked in the gym, on the track or on the basketball court but he also won't be beat in preparation. He will not lose when it comes to the mental approach either.

The Power of the Mind

Once the warrior has spent the time in preparation, the perspiration part is now necessary. This is the time for physical action to complement the mental. But here again, Kobe relies on his gladiator mentality, in approaching physical action.

To simply act without prior thought is wasted movement. Kobe knows what he wants to do physically. He knows ahead of time how he will act, how he will use his body. But, most importantly, Kobe focuses his mind on the task at hand.

While visualization on the part of athletes is used and actually respected, most circles and the average fan, still view the concept as "out there." Hearing that Phil Jackson had the Laker team meditate for 20 minutes before Game 7 of this past year's, 2010, NBA Finals, is laughable and crazy to most people.

But not to the warrior, not to the gladiator, not to the Zen Master and surely, not to Kobe Bryant. He understands what the mental means. He has been with Jackson long enough never to question this aspect of his coaching style. While Kobe will still question a play or decision made by Jackson, he never questions Jackson's mental games.

The proof is on the scoreboard. Eleven tittles. Whatever voodoo or crazy Indian Shaman magic Jackson is preaching, Kobe knows it works.

That is because he too uses it and has since he was a kid. Kobe inherently knew the power of the mind. He somehow understood, long before meeting Phil Jackson, that what you hold in mind, you get. Kobe understood the practice of visualization.

He said, "I love the game. I really do. As a kid, when things were bad for me at school or at home, I would go to the park and envision the dream. You've probably had that same one: I'd be playing for the Lakers, winning championships and hitting the game winning shots. I'd listen to the crowd roar when I put the dagger in the other team's heart, and on the road I'd hear the silence of other teams' arenas. I've actually done these things in my career. But I had done them before, because in my mind and in my heart it felt so real to me. So when I was there I had been there before."

This is a key component of Kobe's mental approach. He is prepared both physically and mentally for all outcomes, all situations. He isn't the best by accident. He's taken the shots in the gym but also in his mind.

At his 2010 Basketball Academy this past summer, Kobe talked about what goes through his mind when he plays. He said the biggest obstacle that you have to overcome when it comes to the mental aspect of the game is self-doubt. What he means is dealing with an opponent is one thing but dealing with yourself, that is what he called "dicey." He said even to this day, he fights that battle in his own mind. He even referred to his play in Game Seven of the 2010 NBA Finals, noting that the key is to constantly think positive and not worry about the mistakes you made.

The true warrior again is focused on the present moment, not concerned about what happened in the past. Kobe again re-emphasized that the biggest battle, the biggest test is always with yourself. The gladiator mentality is to recognize this and push through it. That is the true lesson. It is not that Kobe doesn't have doubts like the rest of us, it's just that he has a heightened awareness of this tendency and makes sure he focuses his mind in the proper direction.

Made Shots, not Taken

To truly understand how Kobe's mind works related to this warrior mentality, the best example will be to learn how Kobe practices.

Most players go to the gym, have a trainer or an assistant coach shag balls. The players takes shots after shot, practicing an array of moves until they become proficient in the shot. Makes perfect sense. And, since the beginning of time, the birth of competitive basketball, players have been training this way. Taking jumpers until they wear out. This is how they improve.

Not Kobe Bryant. Not this warrior. Taking shots is not in Kobe's vocabulary. The subtle difference is the word taken in the earlier sentence.

Kobe doesn't believe in taking shots.

Here's what he said on the matter to Esquire Magazine a few year's back that will help you understand this small but massive difference between Kobe and every other player. The article said:

"A few years ago, Kobe fractured the fourth metacarpal bone in his right hand. He missed the first fifteen games of the season; he used the opportunity to learn to shoot jump shots with his left, which he has been known to do in games. While it was healing, the ring finger, the one just adjacent to the break, spent a lot of time taped to his pinkie. In the end, Kobe discovered, his four fingers were no longer evenly spaced; now they were separated, two and two. As a result, his touch on the ball was different, his shooting percentage went down. Studying the film, he noticed that his shots were rotating slightly to the right.

To correct the flaw, Kobe went to the gym over the summer and made one hundred thousand shots. That's one hundred thousand made, not taken. He doesn't practice taking shots, he explains. He practices making them. If you're clear on the difference between the two ideas, you can start drawing a bead on Kobe Bryant, who may well be one of the most misunderstood figures in sports today. It is a tragic misunderstanding, for his sake and for ours. You can blame it on the press. You can blame it on the way the world revolves around fame and money. You can blame it on Kobe himself."

Made versus Taken. Not just words but a true mental difference. An approach that really does make all the difference. Kobe goes to the gym to make shots. Not take them.

That goes back to the earlier quote from Kobe on preparation. He practices over and over again, so when he is in the game, he's been there before, done it before. He isn't scared nor surprised. He is ready. And, he's ready to make them. He doesn't take a last second shot, he makes one. Whether it finds the bottom of the net or not, the outcome is nearly irrelevant to the warrior.

It is the visualization and most importantly, the expectation. The key here is expectation. When Kobe practices making shots, he then expects making them. When you expect something, it comes. You believe. You begin to know that you know.

That is where Kobe gets with this preparation. He begins to know he will hit a last second shot. He's done it endless times, both in his mind and on the practice court. Success breeds success. And, he gets what he expects. For the warrior, the heart of this principle is that Kobe expects greatness. He expects success.

So, to Kobe Bryant, his journey of a Thousand Miles starts with a thousand jumpers a day.

Master A Piece

Kobe creates masterpieces during games because off the court, when he practices, as he prepares, he breaks each move, each skill down to its most basic and fundamental components. He truly does master a piece at a time.

Here's Lessons from Kobe on various signature and "go to" moves:

Kobe Bryant: Outside Jumper Walkthrough

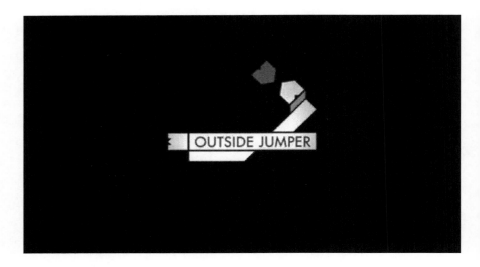

Type the URL Below in your Browser to watch directly from YouTube

http://www.youtube.com/watch?v=6hYlOqa8whk

Kobe Bryant: Pump fake & Pivot Walkthrough

Type the URL Below in your Browser to watch directly from YouTube

http://www.youtube.com/watch?v=e88Z_b756ig

Kobe Bryant: Reverse Lay-up Walkthrough

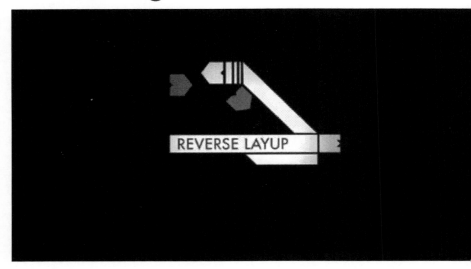

Type the URL Below in your Browser to watch directly from YouTube

http://www.youtube.com/watch?v=8OpWb4Y7QeY

Kobe Bryant: Pull-up Jumper Walkthrough

Type the URL Below in your Browser to watch directly from YouTube

http://www.youtube.com/watch?v=Uz1Kb8Hz620

A Free Lesson With: Kobe Bryant

Type the URL Below in your Browser to watch directly from YouTube

http://www.youtube.com/watch?v=aSqeWUuQSIM&feature=fvw

Be A Patient Warrior

But Kobe had to add one more element over time to his "Victor Mentality." The warrior needed to learn one more key principle and add it to his life. Kobe had to learn the power of patience.

The great warriors are sometimes not only silent but patient. They don't charge headfirst into battle. They are methodical. They are prepared. And, they are patient.

This principle was difficult for Kobe to truly grasp because of his burning desire to be great. The fire that burns in his own belly sometimes spreads and singes those around him. Many times his drive has scorched his teammates. He said recently regarding learning patience the following:

"At times it's frustrating and it tries my patience, but in the beginning years of my career my teammates were patient with me and trusted in the fact that I would figure everything out, so now I must return that favor to this generation of Lakers. This is our challenge, our mountain, and these are my brothers. I must guide them to the point we all want to get to. No matter what."

There is real power in patience. Kobe has finally learned this. While experience has been the true teacher of this principle to Kobe, he has also benefited greatly from the partnership with Coach Jackson.

Phil Jackson embodies patience. There isn't a Laker fan on the planet who hasn't screamed at their TV for Jackson to call a timeout. But, he doesn't. He won't because he is always the beacon of calm. He never is rattled. He wants to teach his players this the only way he knows that can be truly learned. By showing them.

Jackson is always calm in the middle of the storm. He sits there, on his special seat due to his back issues, and appears to be off in some other world, not even paying attention to the game. This might even be why many critics think he doesn't coach. But it is the exact opposite. Jackson is fully present. He is only in the moment. He teaches this principle constantly to his players. He prepares off the court so he can be fully there on.

The key aspect of Jackson's demeanor is patience. He is patient with his team, he is patient with himself. This has rubbed off greatly on Kobe. He has learned the true power of patience and it has made all the difference in his life.

Putting it all Together- The Master working his Craft

Kobe is the best because he truly seems to live his warrior mentality on a daily basis. He walks his own walk.

The best example of learning both Kobe's mental and physical approaches to the game, to his love, is to see it in action. To show, not just be told. So, here is the Master working his Craft.

This is a day in the life of Kobe Bryant, courtesy of an excerpt from *Sports Illustrated*, when they were granted full access with Kobe on a game day.

Commuting to Staples with Kobe Bryant- by Rick Reily, Sports Illustrated

It's 49 miles from Kobe Bryant's house in Orange County to Staples Center and yet, even in a Ferrari, it takes him 10 hours and 16 minutes.

What takes him so long? You're about to ride shotgun and find out:

7:15 a.m. Nearly $140 into a cab ride from my place, a security gate opens at the end of a very swank cul de sac to reveal Kobe Bryant, father of two, standing in front of seven vehicles—the Ferrari, the Range Rover, the Escalade, the Bentley Coupe, the two-door plastic Fred Flintstone car, the training-wheels bike and the tricycle smashed into a bush.

"You ready to go?" he asks. "I hate to be late."

I have a bag and nowhere to put it, since the Ferrari is basically a 503-horsepower engine with two seats. So he takes two helmets out of the trunk and puts the bag in.

Helmets for a car? Uh-oh.

7:21 a.m. I immediately spill my coffee in the $300,000-plus Ferrari, but how was I supposed to know he'd demonstrate its 0 to 60 mph in 3.1-seconds right at the very moment I was about to sip my delicious venti mochachino?

Trying to wipe up the puddle with my sock without him noticing and trying to be heard over the Ferrari's throaty roar, I nearly yell my interview:

Me: "Why are we leaving so early for a 6:30 Clippers game?"

Bryant: "Game day. Lots to do."

Me: "Why does a Los Angeles Laker live clear down in *Weeds* suburbia?"

Bryant: "It's peaceful. It's a better place to bring up kids. Nice people down here."

Me: "What's the fastest you've ever driven this thing?"

Bryant: "We're about to find out."

Me (to self): Did I ever complete my will?

Of course, the 11-time All-Star doesn't always drive to work. Sometimes he has one of his off-duty, armed, Lakers-provided police officers take him in a customized van so he can watch scouting DVDs and ice his feet and knees. (He ices them for 20 minutes three times a day. The man spends more time in ice than Ted Williams.) Occasionally, though, he charters a helicopter. "Sometimes, there's just things you cannot miss," he says.

Like?

"Like my daughter's soccer game. Because what if I miss her first goal?"

Can't say I ever choppered into one of my daughter's soccer games, but still.

Bryant, 30, has been known to get up earlier than many barn owls to conduct his famously brutal workouts. One time, Larry Drew II—who now plays at North Carolina—asked to shadow him on one.

"OK," Kobe said. "Pick you up at 3:30."

But 3:30 came and went and Kobe never showed. Then, at 3:30 the next morning, he was ringing Drew's doorbell.

"You ready?" Kobe asked.

"I like to just get up and get it done," he explained to me, "then I'm back home and nobody's even up. Haven't missed a thing."

7:30 a.m. Bryant pulls the yellow Ferrari up to a massive O.C. health club and leaves it. This will happen many times today, leaving the car right in front of buildings. Gods do not park.

Today is a Sunday and it's bothering him that he'll have to miss coloring with his girls—6 and 2—watching Ariel in "The Little Mermaid" for the 1,003rd time with his girls and going to Disneyland with the girls. But he's obsessed with winning the 2009 NBA title, which means he's committed to his boys. He wants to be as chiseled as possible for the coming playoff pounding. That's why it's no surprise we're met by Tim Grover, Michael Jordan's genius strength and conditioning coach.

Grover puts Bryant through a game-day workout like
I've never seen. (Warning: If you don't want to feel like a
complete jelly-filled donut, don't read this next part.)
Among a dozen other drills, Bryant does suicide push-
ups. At the top of the pushup, he launches himself off
the mat so hard that both his feet come off the ground
and his hands slap his pecs. He does three sets of seven
of these. This makes me turn away and whimper softly.

8:35 a.m. Bryant wheels the asphalt-eating Ferrari
onto the I-405 north and begins answering my
questions about this remarkable comeback he's making
in America, in basketball and in his life, which would be
fascinating, if it weren't for the 70 mph-circus going on
all around us.

People are pulling up next to us and waving. And
screaming. And taking pictures with their cell phones.
And honking. And craning back in their seats to see.
And not watching the road. And getting too damn close.
And Kobe doesn't seem to see any of it.

"Life is really good now," he's saying.

Kobe! Kill 'em tonight! Yeeeeaaahhh bbbboy!

"And it's funny. A lot of these companies who dumped
us during the [sexual assault] trial [in which all charges
were dropped] are calling us now asking us to come
back. And I just kind of smile and go, 'No. No, thanks,
homie. We're good.' But that hurt, dude. To just be
dropped like that. It hurt."

The guy in the Toyota Tundra is signaling that he wants
an autograph.

"But my wife and I, we toughed it out. She and I, we got
through it. We're going to be celebrating our ... "

Two morons are motioning to me that they'd like Kobe
to get off at the next exit and take a picture with them.

" ... eight-year anniversary together. And when I think about how I almost lost it, the family and everything ... "

I can read their lips: "Dude! Please?!"

" ... I'm just very thankful, and blessed. It was really close there for awhile."

Even a Weekly Shopper reporter would follow that answer up with, "What do you mean?" But a knucklehead in a Ford truck is trying to cut in front of us so his buddy can take a picture out of the back window, so I ask, "Do you ever wreck on this commute?"

"No," he says with a grin, "but one time, this one guy was looking back and hit the guy in front of him. Not hard or anything, but he definitely hit the guy. It was kinda funny."

With all that chaos, I can't really vouch for the accuracy of all this, but I'm pretty sure Bryant says:

- He's taken up golf. Played Pelican Hill the other day with Maris Valainis, who played Jimmy Chitwood in *Hoosiers*.
- If I weren't in the car, he'd be listening to Lil Wayne, Jay-Z or Biggie Smalls.
- He loves marketing and advertising. In fact, he conceived and wrote a Carl's Jr. poster, which featured Jerry West, Kareem Abdul-Jabbar and himself, and the slogan: "They Who Endure, Conquer."
- He and his wife, Vanessa, have no nannies.
- Most sports talk radio makes him nauseous.
- He's addicted to Discovery Channel, loves to spear fish and reads New York Times columnist Thomas Friedman.
- He has no plans to opt out of his contract at the end of this season, but "you can never absolutely say no, right?"

- His daughters speak a mix of English, Spanish and Italian.
- He'd like to have a boy.

Forty minutes, 37 missed quotes and 118 gawkers later, we've gone the 43 miles from the health club in O.C. to the Lakers' practice facility in El Segundo, right near LAX, for shootaround. He pulls up to the spot in front of the door, gets out of the car and doesn't lock it. It's all I can do not to get on my knees and kiss the ground.

12:03 p.m. After his two hours of shooting and stretching, we're off to a downtown hotel, where Kobe will ice, shower, sleep, eat (it's always the same: chicken, rice and broccoli), watch scouting DVDs and make calls until it's time to go. This time we're following one of the off-duty cops, who's driving the gray van.

"Why are we following the cop?" I ask.

"Because I need my jug to ice," he says.

"So why don't we take it ourselves?" I ask.

"Won't fit."

Do you love it? His ice jug gets a police escort.

"What if you can't sleep at the hotel?" I ask as he leadfoots it up the 110 north. "What do you do? Walk around downtown L.A.?"

He laughs and looks at me like I just landed from the planet Nimrod.

"Uh, no. I can't walk around L.A. There are fans and then there are LAKER fans. LAKER fans are, like, 10 times more into it than regular fans."

Example: One time, he met a man who had the exact same tattoos as him. Literally, the exact same tattoos, down to the size, color, font, style, even the names of his daughters, his wife, the Bible verses, the crown, everything. And this was in Ohio.

"I mean, what do you say to something like that?" he says, still amazed. "I'm like, 'Wow.' And then I whispered to my security guy, 'Get his social security, OK?'"

12:14 p.m. Four security guards are waiting for us at the hotel. We leave the Ferrari AND the van out front, go through a side entrance, up a freight elevator, to a suite that's waiting for him...

Read the entire article. Type the URL below into your browser.

http://sports.espn.go.com/espnmag/story?id=4068270

Apply the Code in Your Own Life

So, ask yourself:

Where can I learn to be more patient in my own life?

Where am I not calm? When do I panic?

Are there times when I could choose to be silent rather than speak?

How can I use this principle to prepare in my own life?

What are my own strengths, and weaknesses?

Can I view my own actions as a neutral observer, without attachment?

How can I use the power of visualization more in my own life?

What am I holding in mind? What I want or what I don't want?

Do I try or simply do?

Do I approach my work as taking or actually making?

Begin to take the necessary steps in your own life to master a piece of your craft, one step at a time and you will be applying this seventh principle.

PRINCIPLE EIGHT

Live With Passion

"What I have come to learn is that my desire to win, the will to pursue my goals with the highest level of intensity and passion, defines me."

What separates someone who doesn't like their job or career and someone who does? What is the common thread that links all great warriors? What is it that allows some artists, composers, or musicians to create masterpieces?

The answer to personal fulfillment and success is what all the greats possessed: Passion.

Leonardo DaVinci doesn't paint the Mona Lisa, regarded as one of the greatest paintings of all-time, without dripping with passion for his art. Michelangelo took something like four years to paint the ceiling of the Sistine Chapel in Rome. It too is considered a masterpiece.

Again, how do these greats create on such a level of excellence?

Passion. Their bodies pulse with a burning desire to fulfill their goals. They ooze their craft and drive themselves to be the greatest, truly create masterpieces.

While it might be a stretch to directly compare a basketball player like Kobe Bryant, or even Michael Jordan, to some of the greatest creators of all-time, we can look at the common traits they all exhibit.

And, the one characteristic displayed by all of them is passion. This is why Passion is a key part of this principle and seems to be one of the fundamental pillars he lives by. Kobe does everything regarding basketball with passion. To him, the sport is his canvas and he is working on painting a masterpiece.

Kobe trains, eats, practices, and plays with passion. While the media classifies him as aloof, obsessed, that is a great error. Kobe is simply misunderstood.

He said, "What I have come to learn is that my desire to win, the will to pursue my goals with the highest level of intensity and passion, defines me."

If you want to truly know what makes Kobe great, what really separates him from all the other NBA players and places him in the upper echelon of the greats of all time, it is passion. He has it. He can't deny it and it can't be denied within him, either. Kobe is borderline obsessed with basketball. And, that is not unique for someone who lives with real passion.

If we were to get TV reports on DaVinci or Michelangelo from back in the day, it would seem like they too were so narrowly focused, so driven, that we'd think something was wrong with them. DaVinci ate, slept and breathed his art. If he wasn't painting, he was drawing. If he wasn't drawing, he was inventing. If he wasn't inventing, he was thinking about it. He was obsessed.

It seems the key component of this Passion Principle is that all the great's level of passion bordered on obsession.

This is a key point to be made. To the warrior, you take what you do, your art and push it to that line, even over it, to blur the focus to the gray area of obsession. So, to be truly great, passion is not just needed but required.

Know Your Real Purpose & Do What You Love

How is it that Kobe can go into the hostile arena of a hated opponent and nail a last second shot when sixteen thousand fans are rooting against him?

This happens not just from focus or only practice. It is again his passion. Kobe seems to understand this principle. And, it appears he has applied it to his life.

Kobe knows his true purpose. He was born to play basketball. He is truly aware of this gift and wants to not waste it but rather, take it to the max. And, he is solely set on being the best.

Most people don't even like to exercise or when they do, they complain about it. Even other NBA players don't want to work hard or simply do just enough to get by. Not Kobe. He loves basketball, loves every aspect of his sport. To him, this is not work. This is fun. This is living your passion.

This is exactly the reason when he plays a road game, he gives his all. He does this in a pre-season game, in one of those long days of February games, and he brings 100% in a playoff battle. That's because he knows that the real warrior must always gives his all. Always.

This is what defines a true gladiator. They know that there are no days, no games, no seconds off. So, when Kobe is playing against a team and crowd who are against him, he doesn't care. He knows he will give his all and that will be enough, at least to him. And, no matter if you love or hate the warrior, we all can see when someone loves what they are doing. Anyone can spot true passion.

Think about it in your own life, in the circles of the relationships around you. You know those individuals who love their job or profession. And, exactly the opposite, you can name on two fingers all the friends of yours who hate their work.

This is because passion and misery have telltale signs. They appear not just in words or complaining or succeeding but in actions. Show don't tell. That is a golden rule in storytelling.

But that also applies in life. People will show you how they truly feel, their real attitude toward say their job, even if they say something otherwise. That's because their actions speak truth, even if their words contradict.

So, even when say a Boston Celtic crowd, who hate the Lakers to their core, watch Kobe playing his heart out, they can respect his effort. That is because great fans know real passion and even if we don't like the player or the team, we still respect him.

Kobe alluded to this exact fact in an interview. He said, "When we play on the road and the entire crowd is booing me it doesn't bother me at all. What I think about is simple: When these fans leave this game I want them to remember how hard I fought and the passion and drive with which I played."

He doesn't hold back. No great warrior does. They can't. It is not in their makeup. They won't cheat their profession, they won't cheat their teammates and, most importantly, they won't cheat themselves.

This is even the reason you see NBA players who are friends off the court go to battle like it is life or death on it. That puzzles the average person. They don't understand this. But the real warrior knows this to his core. So does Kobe. One simple reason. Passion. Period.

KOBE: Live With Honor – Determination

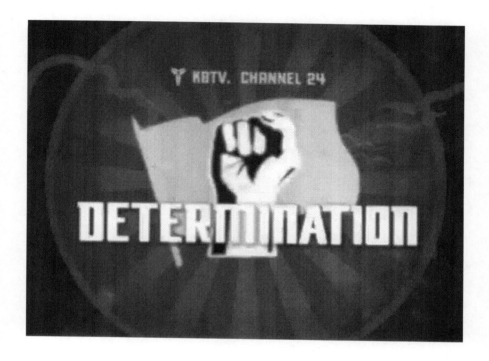

Type the URL Below in your Browser to watch directly from YouTube
http://www.youtube.com/watch?v=_yMzvKzttZE&feature=related

Make Every Second Count

Kobe understands how precious time is. He knows that the warrior's life is to never stop, use every second, and make it all count.

If you ever wondered why Kobe changed his jersey number from 8 to 24, the essence is in making every hour count. At his 2009 Basketball Academy, he explained the jersey switch. He said at this stage of his basketball career, it really is all about taking each day as it comes and enjoying each moment. He said he really didn't realize how fast his career had gone, how everything was nearly a blur. He might not have truly appreciated everything. That is why he switched to 24. It is symbolic to him to take each day as it comes and take one day at a time.

The warrior only lives in the moment. Period.

How Privileged to Watch Them Play

It seems like the greats are never here long enough. We wish their careers could last forever. That's why we never want them to retire. We can't get enough and hope they will always be playing. But they don't.

Bill Russell seemed to own the NBA as his Boston Celtics won title after title in the 1960's but he retired. Gone. Magic Johnson owned the eighties, playing in eight out of ten NBA Finals during that decade. He and Larry Bird were the faces of the NBA. Their gifts on display almost every night, mesmerizing us, and letting us cheer their greatness. And, then, like a rainstorm, they were gone. Michael Jordan simply dazzled us. Early in his career, it seemed like he really could fly, could hang in mid-air. And then, he started winning titles and seemed like he couldn't be beat. His play was breathtaking and he dominated the 1990's. But, then, he too was gone.

Hear this and let it really sink in. Kobe will not be here forever. But right now, this moment, we are truly witnesses, privileged to greatness, just like when the legends of the past played. Kobe is a gladiator giving his all each night in the arena, ready to die, his passion dripping from his jersey along with his sweat. He said once the following, which goes to the heart of his passion:

"Even though those fans may chant "Kobe sucks", when they leave that arena I want them to walk out with a different feeling than they came in with. When they leave they'll leave with the understanding that they have just witnessed a player give himself completely to his passion; they have just watched an athlete pour every ounce of his heart and soul out on that floor. And hopefully, when the next volume of my life is all said and done, they will respect and appreciate the years that I spent giving all of me to the game that means everything to me."

So, whether you love, like, or even hate him, you have to cherish this talent. Because soon enough, this great warrior will step away, will leave the game that he has given so much, the sport that he loves, the battles that defines him. Like the others before him, Kobe too will be gone. And, that will be a sad day.

Apply the Code in Your Own Life

Ask yourself these questions regarding this Principle:

What is your true passion in life?

What fills you up, what activity would you do if money didn't matter?

Where are you holding back in your life, not giving your all?

Who around you in your life is living with true passion? And, who isn't?

What do you love to do so much you border on obsession doing it?

Can you truly live with passion in your life. If you can say "yes" to that, then you embody this eighth and final principle.

POST-GAME

" Scito hoc super omnia....Tempus neminem non manet....Carpe diem."

The above quote is more Latin from Kobe. It means, "Know this above all else.... Fully use every point, moment, and hour that you have. Time waits for no man.... Seize the day."

Kobe is quoted saying this mantra often, it is written on his website, even on products he endorses. That's because he wants to seize each moment. He knows he is blessed. He understands what is required to be great. And, he is willing to do both the mental and physical work to achieve his burning desires, make his goals reality. But he also knows that this moment, this amazing career, won't last forever. So, Kobe makes every day count.

And, while we view Kobe as only a basketball great, have seen in detail the level of commitment to his sport, what he gives and bleeds to stand on top of the mountain, Kobe is much more than just a basketball player. Far more.

Kobe is a family man. Many people may not want to hear that, or believe it. They still judge the young, twenty-something who must of did something awful in Colorado. They say, hold the old line, that no matter what happened in that hotel room, the guy is no good because he cheated on this wife. Well, Kobe admitted to the mistake he made. And, we all make mistakes. We all fall down. It is not in the failing that we find growth but in the getting back up.

Kobe has been knocked down, more times than we can even know and not only the ones that have been publicized, but Kobe has gotten back up, dusted himself off and gone at it again. This is the way of the warrior. Keep going. Never stop. Don't settle.

Kobe is as driven to be a great family man, good husband and wonderful dad as he is focused to be one of the greatest basketball players of all time.

Kobe has a loving and supportive wife and two wonderful young daughters. He adores them. After every home game, as Kobe exits the arena, finished from the battle, dripping in sweat, having either won or lost, he disappears into the tunnel that leads to the Lakers' locker room, in the belly of the Staples Center. But before Kobe reaches that player sanctuary, each night, his wife and daughters await him. He first kisses his wife, and then hugs both girls. For a moment, the warrior is gone, replaced by a normal person, just a man, with his family.

These are sweet moments for Kobe. His girls are his world. All three of them. When he isn't playing, isn't training, he's with them. He brings them to his battles, they cheer his highs and give him solace for his lows.

They are the constants in his life. You will even see him bring his daughters onto the podium during a post-game interview. This is the softer side of Kobe, the gladiator, the relaxed warrior. Not too long ago, the up and coming, striving to fit in Kobe Bryant, would never have let his family near him after a game. That would be exposing to much of himself, opening him up to letting his opponents see his weakness, discover his loves, know his vulnerabilities.

And, Kobe is vulnerable. He is just an ordinary man blessed with extraordinary skill and mindset. But outward achievements count for nothing in the end. Kobe understands this. A true warrior does. That is why he is about Honor and Love. Those are the things that are everlasting.

Monuments and trophies, when you're gone, are empty. But who you were, how you lived and, most importantly, what, who and how you loved is all that matters. And, Kobe loves something even more than basketball. He loves his family.

At his 2010 Basketball Academy this past summer, Kobe was asked how he likes to relax off the court. He said after a game, he'll go home and play with his kids, who are normally still up. He joked saying he gets beat up for forty-eight minutes during a game but then will go home and will be a human jungle gym, playing with his girls. That's how warriors relax.

But, he also loves another sport almost equal to hoop.

The Second Sport He Loves

Kobe can't get enough of futbol, or soccer. He fell in love with the sport when he lived in Italy and is an avid fan to this day. If you want to know what Kobe does outside of the game, beside spending time with his family, he loves soccer. He eats it up. He watches games, reads articles, tracks his favorite players. His extracurricular activity, his true hobby, is soccer.

At Kobe's 2010 Basketball Academy, he talked about Spain, World Cup and soccer. He said he still loves soccer, it is truly is second favorite sport. His favorite player used to be Ronaldinho but now it is Messi. Kobe said learning to play soccer as a kid definitely prepared him for basketball, specifically helping with his footwork, timing, and footspeed. He also predicted Spain would win the World Cup, which they did. The man knows his futbol.

Check out the following video and you'll see why.

Kobe Bryant & World Cup 2010

Type the URL Below in your Browser to watch directly from YouTube

http://www.youtube.com/watch?v=Gl5OrhyFfoI&feature=related

Kobe wore the number 10 when he played in the 2008 Olympics because the number has meaning to him in soccer. The greats, at least to him, wore the same number. Pele, Maradona, and Rondalihno use that number.

For those that don't know the sport, Pele is the Babe Ruth of soccer. The first true great. This Brazilian owned the game in the sixties and seventies and was a true magician with the soccerball. He was also a winner and took the sport to the next level.

Maradona played for Argentina and would be the Charles Barkley of the game, except that Maradona also won a World Cup, unlike Barkley who never won a NBA Title. Maradona was both talented and controversial. He is best known as a passionate player, who was responsible for one of the most famous plays in all of soccer history. During the 1986 World Cup, Maradona scored a goal not with his feet but his fist. Near the net, he went up to head the ball but ended up hitting the soccerball with his clenched fist, not his forehead. The referees missed the call and the goal stood. But on replay, it was clear that the Argentinean had cheated, had touched the ball with his hand, which is illegal in soccer. The play became known as "The Hand of God."

Rondalihno is currently arguably one of soccer's greatest players. He is from Brazil and plays on their national team for World Cups. He also plays during the year for one of the best clubs in the world, AC Milan.

Kobe loves these players and loves soccer. He attended the World Cup in South Africa in the summer of 2010, even though he was tired from just winning the NBA championship less than a month before. He traveled to Africa to attend as many games as he could.

Soccer is also one of the common threads, along with the Spanish language, between Kobe and his teammate, Pau Gasol. The Spaniard understands and loves soccer as much as Kobe. The only difference between these two Lakers is that Kobe is not passionate about the Spanish national team, and Gasol is.

Kobe also has other interests outside basketball. He likes to travel with his family, mostly to a place he is very familiar with: Europe. Many summers Kobe takes his family to both Italy and Spain, places he loves and feels comfortable.

Kobe also enjoyed his worldwide fame during the 2008 Olympics. The player with the top jersey sales worldwide, Kobe Bryant, treated the Chinese people to a firsthand meeting of their idol. He is beloved in China and traveled there again this past summer of 2010.

Kobe also enjoys movies and books. One of his favorite books is *Blink*, by Malcolm Gladwell. In this popular book, the author describes the main subject of his book as "think slicing," which he says is our ability to gauge what is really important from a very narrow period experience. No wonder Kobe is drawn to such a book. It is all about the power of the mind.

At his 2010 Basketball Academy this past summer, Kobe said his favorite movie right now is *The Hangover* and one of his best movies of all-time is *The Wedding Crashers*. Obviously, the movie *Gladiator* also ranks at the top of Kobe's list, if we go by the words on his website.

The Benjamin's- The Number's Game of Kobe

Kobe is not only one of the top paid players in the NBA, but he also has a slew of endorsement deals that add to his pocketbook. While he went through a serious dry spell after the Colorado incident, where various sponsors and endorsers dropped him or didn't re-sign him to new contracts, that is long past.

Kobe is the NBA's most popular player worldwide. While LeBron James has supplanted Kobe as the top athlete in the USA, Kobe still reigns over the globe. This is due to the fact that the Chinese love and adore him and with that country's numbers of diehard basketball fans, they add to Kobe's lead each year.

The Chinese love Kobe because he wins. They reward and hold excellence on the highest of pedestals. That is why LeBron will never have China in his corner until he wins a NBA Championship. Kobe is a winner and because of that, the Chinese buy up anything and everything he sells. Kobe's jersey sales top LeBron, Dwyane Wade and all others globally.

And, with Kobe's resurgence in popularity, so came the endorsements. But Kobe has a long memory and those companies that abandoned him or dropped him after his personal problems in 2004, he remembers. He hasn't re-signed with any of those companies, even when they have thrown massive money his way. That is because a warrior remembers.

He still plays the sponsor game but with honor. Kobe's list of current endorsement deals read like a who's who of top companies. Forbes Magazine states that Kobe receives approximately $25 million from endorsement deals. Of course, there is footwear giant, Nike, who has created and entire line and ad campaign around the Black Mamba. But Kobe also rakes in money from Panini trading cards, Vitamin Water and some special deals exclusive to China.

In 2010, Kobe topped over $30 million from sponsors, which is the first time an NBA player surpassed $30 mil since Michael Jordan did it in 1998. This proves that Kobe is on the top of his game, even off the court.

The Future- Life After Hoop

What Kobe will do beyond basketball is anyone's guess. He might end up going into business, following another Laker great, Magic Johnson. Or, with his knowledge, he might end up in the broadcast booth. Or, he might simply ride off into the sunset.

At his 2010 Basketball Academy this past summer, he broached this exact subject. He was asked specifically what he would do after he retires. Kobe answered saying he still had a ways to go, still had things he wanted to do. He said he might do more basketball camps but he would never coach. He also said he might go into business. There have already been and will continue to be opportunities that open up for him in the business arena. And, sure, when that times comes, he'll shift his focus to those new ventures. But, he reminded everyone, right now, he is still one hundred percent focused on basketball.

That's the Gladiator mentality at its finest. Still focused only on the task at hand, locked into the present moment. That's because this warrior possesses the skills and knowledge to be successful at whatever he puts his mind and focus upon.

But right now, the future isn't here. If Kobe knows one thing, has learned anything from Phil Jackson, if he truly lives his Gladiator mentality, he doesn't care about tomorrow. He is focused only on the moment, as a great warrior will do.

That's why Kobe takes it one day at a time. He lives by his own warrior ways and always remembers to *Seize the Day*.

Hopefully, after learning about Kobe's life, you can too.

BIBILIOGRAPHY

Archer, Todd. Caron Butler grateful he was Kobe Bryant's teammate. http://mavsblog.dallasnews.com/archives/2010/02/caron-butler-grateful-he-was-kobe-bryant.html. Dallas. Dallas News. 2010.

Bandenhausen, Kurt. *Kobe Bryant: King of the Court.* New York. Forbes Magazine/Forbes.com. 2010.

Bryant, Kobe. *Various quotations.* www.kb24.com. Kobe's official website. 2010.

Bryant, Kobe. *In His Own Words.* New York. Dime Magazine. 2006. Edition #22.

Gametime Workouts. Kobe Bryant and his Devil Workout. Gametimeworkouts.com. January 2008. (http://www.gametimeworkouts.com/2008/01/kobe-bryant-and-his-devil-routine.html)

Guarneri, Brandon. *Kobe Bryant.* New York. Men's Fitness. 2006.

Inside Hoops. Kobe Bryant's 666 Workout. www.
Insidehoops.com. August 2006.
http://www.insidehoops.com/forum/showthread.php?t=930
5

Jenkins, Lee. Dynasty: Beginning or Ending? New York.
Sports Illustrated. June 2010.

MacMullan, Jackie. *Kobe Bryant: Imitating Greatness*.
Connecticut. ESPN.com. June 2010.

Odeven, Ed. *Dad says conditioning key for Kobe.* Tokyo.
Hoop Scoop/The Japan Times Ltd. 2007.

Reily, Rick. *Commuting to Staples with Kobe Bryant*.
Connecticut. ESPN The Magazine. April 2009.

Sager, Mike. *Kobe Bryant Doesn't Want Your Love*. New
York. Esquire Magazine. 2007. November issue.

TopBuzz. *Kobe Now a Sleek Corvette*. Posted by
JamFan. 2005. http://lakers.topbuzz.com/a-4.html

Wikipedia. *Kobe Bryant.*
http://en.wikipedia.org/wiki/Kobe_bryant. 2010.

About the Author

Pat Mixon is a sportswriter and Featured Columnist for one of the largest sports websites in the U.S., The Bleacher Report.com. His articles are also read on Bleacher Report partners such as LA Times, CBS Sports.com, and USA Today, to just name a few.

Pat Mixon is an avid basketball fan, having both played and followed the sport for nearly 20 years. He loves all things basketball, including college and the NBA but his real love and passion are the Los Angeles Lakers, having been a fan of the Purple and Gold since his youth.

When Pat isn't watching, playing or writing about basketball, he is hard at work on his first fiction novel, a Sports thriller. Pat lives in California with his wife.

Visit Pat's website at http://www.patmixon.com/ for bonus materials, additional videos, and other information.

This book is also available as an e-Book at most online retailers.

9604719R0

Made in the USA
Lexington, KY
12 May 2011